An Instant Guide to
BIRDS

Nearly 200 of the most common
North American birds
described and illustrated in full color

MIKE LAMBERT AND ALAN PEARSON

GRAMERCY BOOKS
NEW YORK

Copyright © 1985 by Atlantis Publications Ltd.
Copyright © 1985 text and illustrations M. Lambert and A. Pearson
All rights reserved under International and Pan-American
Copyright Conventions.

No part of this book may be reproduced or transmitted in any form or by any
means electronic or mechanical including photocopying, recording, or by
any information storage and retrieval system, without permission in writing
from the publisher.

This 1999 edition is published by Gramercy Books™
an imprint of Random House Value Publishing, Inc.,
201 East 50th Street, New York, New York 10022.

Gramercy Books™ and colophon are trademarks of
Random House Value Publishing, Inc.

Random House
New York • Toronto • London • Sydney • Auckland
http://www.randomhouse.com/

Printed and bound in Malaysia

Library of Congress Cataloging-in-Publication Data

Lambert, Mike, 1945–
        An instant guide to birds : nearly 200 of the most common North
    American birds described and illustrated in full color / Mike Lambert
    and Alan Pearson.
            p.   cm.
        Originally published: New York : Bonanza Books, 1985.
        Includes bibliographical references (p.   ) and index.
        ISBN 0-517-46891-3
        1. Birds—United States—Identification. 2. Birds—United
    States—Pictorial Works. I. Pearson, Alan, 1960–   . II. Title.
    QL682.L36   1999
    598'.0973—dc21   98-29074
                                                                    CIP

15 14 13

Contents

INTRODUCTION   4

HOW TO USE THIS BOOK   5

GLOSSARY OF TERMS   8

THE PARTS OF A BIRD   9

SECTION 1:   10

BIRDS OF TOWN
Regular visitors to yards, suburban areas and city parks

SECTION 2:   51

BIRDS OF COUNTRY
Farms and woods, desert and prairie, wild country and mountains

SECTION 3:   88

BIRDS OF WATER
Inland waterways and estuaries, coasts and sea

SECTION 4:   118

LESS COMMON SPECIES

INDEX AND CHECK-LIST   126

Introduction

The chief aim of this book is to enable the reader, and newcomer to birdwatching, to identify positively and as simply as possible the great majority of birds which he is likely to encounter.

We all come into contact with birds, most of us with more interest and curiosity than specialist knowledge. This simple pocket-sized guide will enable you to identify a bird seen on a country walk, on holiday, or a visitor to the yard, and will add to the casual observer's knowledge of common bird species.

There is, to be sure, no shortage of books on birds, but most of them group birds in families which makes identification a confusing and time-consuming process. A bird is unlikely to wait around and pose helpfully while the enthusiastic beginner leafs through an entire list of birds in the hope of identifying the species before him. If he has little or no idea which family a particular bird might belong to, where is he to begin?

Similarly it is often difficult to establish from traditional guides whether a bird is a real rarity or merely a little uncommon. Thus it would be a simple error to decide that a lightweight sea bird with a black body and a buoyant flight action was a White-winged Tern when it was in fact the far more common Black Tern. *An Instant Guide to Birds* avoids confusion by editing out rarities such as the White-winged Tern.

Only the most common species have been featured and it is worth stressing that these are not necessarily the most common in terms of numbers, but those that the non-expert beginner is most likely to meet. So birds that are shy of humans or that are found only in inaccessible or very localized regions have been omitted, since they are only rarely seen by the great majority of observers.

The very size and the diversity of climate and geography of the North American continent produces a rich and varied bird population and also highlights a strong east/west division, roughly following the line of the Rockies. The huge distances or the presence of the Rockies separate similar species so that their ranges rarely overlap. If one is common and the other rare, only the common one is shown, e.g. Scarlet and Western Tanagers.

So you will not have to go out of your way to see any of the birds featured here and with the help of this simple identification guide you will, we hope, increase and expand your interest and knowledge.

Most of the more unusual species are listed in group color plates in the Less Common Species section (pp 118-125). If you regularly see species from this additional selection, then you have probably outgrown this book and should seek more specialist guides.

How to use this book

To enable the newcomer to birdwatching to make a positive identification as simply as possible, we have divided the birds into sections according to the type of location where you are **most** likely to see them.

If, for instance, you want to identify a bird seen on a walk in the city park, you should consult the section headed **Birds of Town**. Each section, that is each type of habitat, is clearly distinguished by the different colored bands at the top of each page (see Fig. 1). Of course, birds are "travelers," so if in any doubt, look at the other habitat sections.

Within each of these sections, birds are not ordered by family but by size, since it is grouping by family that makes most bird guides so difficult for beginners to follow. So, knowing where you saw the bird and having turned to the appropriate section, you need to make a rough guess at its size.

How big was the bird?

Birds are featured in order of size from smallest to largest and the relative size category is denoted by a symbol at the top of each page beside the name of the bird (see Fig. 2). This means that two birds of the same family may be separated by a bird or birds of intermediate size. For example, six of our commonest Woodpeckers will be found as follows: Downy Woodpecker at

Fig. 1. Locating the bird

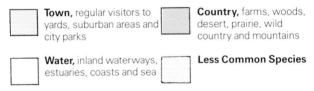

Town, regular visitors to yards, suburban areas and city parks

Country, farms, woods, desert, prairie, wild country and mountains

Water, inland waterways, estuaries, coasts and sea

Less Common Species

Fig. 2. Guide to bird sizes
All sizes refer to the length of the bird, from bill-tip to tail-end.

Tiny
3½-5in

Small
5¼-7in

Medium
7½-10in

Medium-large
10½-15½in

Large
16-25in

Very large
26-47in

6½in, Yellow-bellied Sapsucker at 8½in, Red-headed Woodpecker at 9in, Hairy Woodpecker at 9½in, Northern Flicker at 12½in and Pileated Woodpecker at 17in.

By flicking through the book you have quickly narrowed the field down to birds of a particular size in a particular location. The information you need to make a positive identification is contained in the colored boxes beneath the illustration of each bird. A specimen page is shown in Fig. 3.

Distinguishing marks

The first box describes the feature or combination of features that are unique to that bird of that size range. In other words, if you are certain of these features, which are also borne out by the color illustration, you have already *positively identified* the bird and need read on only out of interest and to build up a more detailed picture of it.

If you are uncertain about these specific features, then the second box completes the description. The third box adds localities and typical habits. However, the second and third boxes, although they provide additional information, do not specifically identify the particular bird. Only the first box can do that.

The fourth box on each page gives the names of similar birds with which the featured bird could be confused. All these "Lookalikes" are either featured in detail themselves or appear under the heading of **Less common species** in section 4.

Lookalikes

This Lookalikes box is important for two reasons. Firstly it is all too easy to jump to conclusions when looking for known identifying features. You can, in effect, already have made up your mind about the bird's identity before checking its specific features in the top box. Check the Lookalikes carefully. Size is easily misjudged and buff plumage, for instance, often mistaken for yellow. This box will give you other possibilities to consider.

Secondly, it is very important for the observer to be aware of exactly what points he should be looking for, as a means of quickly distinguishing similar birds. This is where guesswork ends and skill begins.

After the three sections of birds featured individually according to typical habitat, section 4 is a grouping, again in strictly size order, of other species which are likely to be observed by non-experts. No text accompanies the illustrations, just the name and size of each species, with its distinguishing features pinpointed.

Before you set out, it is worth emphasizing that birds are not glued to their habitat and may travel widely. The habitat divisions in this book indicate the most likely location for each bird. But be prepared to consider information on localities and habits in the third box, if you feel sure that you have seen a bird out of habitat. Any usual variations will be listed.

Suddenly a bird is disturbed in front of you. How big was it? Always err slightly on the small size. If you think it was the size of an American Robin (10in), start with the 8-9in long birds and progress through the pages until you see the one that looks similar. Check the first box containing the specific features. If it tallies with what you have seen, you have identified the bird from a minimum of detail. The second, third and Lookalike boxes should reinforce your identification and also make you aware of similar birds with different specific features.

Good birdwatching, and don't forget to check your sightings on the check-list provided with the index!

Fig. 3. Specimen Page

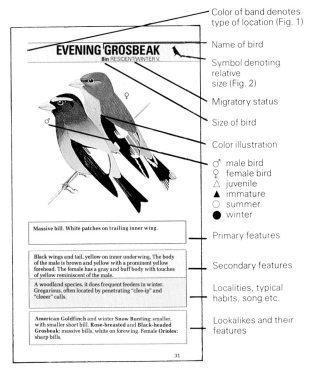

Color of band denotes type of location (Fig. 1)

EVENING GROSBEAK
8in RESIDENT/WINTER V.

Name of bird

Symbol denoting relative size (Fig. 2)

Migratory status

Size of bird

Color illustration

♂ male bird
♀ female bird
△ juvenile
▲ immature
○ summer
● winter

Massive bill. White patches on trailing inner wing.

Primary features

Black wings and tail, yellow on inner underwing. The body of the male is brown and yellow with a prominent yellow forehead. The female has a gray and buff body with touches of yellow reminiscent of the male.

A woodland species, it does frequent feeders in winter. Gregarious, often located by penetrating "clee-ip" and "cleeer" calls.

Secondary features

Localities, typical habits, song etc.

American Goldfinch and winter Snow Bunting: smaller, with smaller short bill. Rose-breasted and Black-headed Grosbeak: massive bills, white on forewing. Female Orioles: sharp bills.

Lookalikes and their features

31

7

Glossary of terms

Adult A mature bird capable of breeding.

Bar A relatively narrow band of color across the area described, e.g. wing bars on a Vireo.

Bib A distinctively colored patch between throat and breast e.g. Black-capped and Carolina Chickadees.

Call A few notes, or even a single note, indicating alarm or acting as a simple statement of presence.

Crest Erectile feathers on the crown, usually prominent during display.

Display A ritualized pattern of behavior, usually movement, by which birds communicate, particularly during courtship and in defense of territory.

Form Separate subspecies of the same species, e.g. Northern Oriole has "Baltimore" and "Bullock's" forms.

Immature A fully grown bird not yet old enough to breed, often in plumage markedly different from the adult.

Internal migrant Species present throughout the year within North America, but with the population showing consistent migration according to the seasons, e.g. Savannah Sparrow.

Juvenile A young bird in its own first plumage variation, having left the nest but not completed its first molt at the end of summer.

Mask A distinctively colored patch of feathers about the eyes, often joined, if only thinly, across the forehead, e.g. Loggerhead Shrike.

Migratory Any species exhibiting movement consistent with the change of seasons is a migratory species.

Patch An area of color, perhaps in the wing, e.g. Northern Mockingbird.

Range That area which contains the vast proportion of the population of the species considered.

Resident Present throughout the year, e.g. House Sparrow; the local population may be supplemented by partial migrants from adjoining areas.

Shield A structure, lacking feathers, on the forehead of some water birds, e.g. American Coot.

Song A sustained and consistent collection of notes used principally to proclaim ownership of territory, particularly during the breeding season.

Spatulate Having a long, spread and flattened shape, e.g. the bill of the Northern Shoveler.

Species A group of individuals (population) whose members resemble each other more closely than they resemble members of other populations and which, almost invariably, are capable of breeding only amongst themselves.

Speculum A panel on the trailing edge of the inner wing feathers of ducks, usually highly and distinctively colored, e.g. Mallard.

Stripe A relatively narrow, long band of color along the area described, e.g. wing stripe on a Spotted Sandpiper.

Subspecies A group of individuals within a species which differ slightly, usually in plumage, from the typical form but which are capable of breeding with any individual of that species.

Summer visitor A migratory species, arriving in spring and returning to its winter home at the end of the breeding season, e.g. Barn Swallow.

Winter visitor A migratory species, arriving in late fall and returning to its summer home to breed when conditions there improve in spring, e.g. Snow Goose.

Fig. 4. The parts of a bird

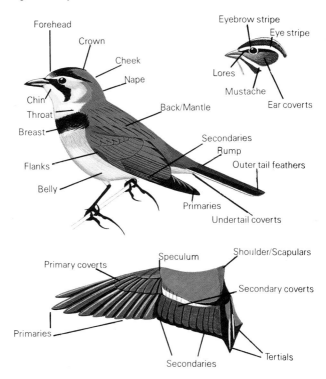

RUBY-THROATED HUMMINGBIRD
SUMMER VISITOR **3¾in**

Only hummingbird seen in the east. Male: red-throated, cleft tail. Female and juveniles: nearly white underparts with buff flanks, no red in tail.

Green head, back and wings, whitish below. Both sexes have a green tail but the female's is blunt-ended with black and white outer tail spots. The bill is medium length for a hummingbird and straight.

Typically this tiny hummingbird hovers drinking nectar from flowers through its specially adapted bill. The wings move so rapidly as to blur. The male performs an aerial "pendulum" display, swinging side to side. Gardens, woodland edges.

Rufous Hummingbird: red in tail feathers. **Black-chinned Hummingbird:** male has violet throat and blunt tail, female has greenish flanks and blunt tail.

♂

Able to move about on tree trunks in any direction.
Rufous underparts.

Dark cap and eye stripe are separated by a bold white
eyebrow stripe. The back and wings are blue-gray.

Seen moving around restlessly in forests or suburban
gardens with mature trees, these attractive little birds are
often in association with chickadees and kinglets. Stumpy-
tailed, they have a jerky awkward flight. Eat insects and nuts.

White-breasted Nuthatch: white-breasted. **Brown Creeper:**
ascends tree trunks. White below, curved bill.

Cocked tail. Lacks prominent eye stripe, back or belly bars.

A large gray wren. Brown above and paler below, with heavy barring on the wings and tail. When close this wren has a distinctive light eye ring.

Common in woods, thickets and gardens, this bird seeks insects in low cover. Small-sized with a disproportionately powerful voice.

Carolina, Bewick's Wrens: have prominent eye stripes.
Brown Creeper: stiff tail, not cocked.

White cheeks, black cap and bib. Black-capped is the northerly species with light patch on inner wing. Carolina is the south-easterly species without the light patch.

White breast, buff flanks and belly. Above, the back is pale gray with tail and wings darker.

Cheeky and acrobatic, these welcome residents frequently visit suburbs and feeders. Otherwise inhabitants of woodland and thickets, their distinctive song "chick-a-dee-dee-dee" locates them.

Bushtits, Nuthatches, Kinglets, Tufted Titmouse and **Blue-gray Gnatcatcher**: all lack bibs.

YELLOW WARBLER
SUMMER VISITOR **5in**

Yellow or yellow-green almost overall. Even the tail spots are yellow.

The male's breast shows bold reddish streaks. Immatures are duller than the adult females and might be confused with Wilson's Warbler and Yellowthroat, but the tail will distinguish. Note the slim insect-eating bill.

A widespread and common summer visitor, this species prefers wet habitats, from swamps to woods and streamsides to gardens. It is noted for its bright clear song.

Wilson's Warbler, female **Yellowthroat** and all other similar Warblers lack yellow tail spots. Female **American Redstart:** has yellow areas at side of tail. **American Goldfinch:** seed-eating bill, black wings.

Seed-eating bill. Unstreaked body plumage. **Male:** black crown and yellow back. **Female:** greenish brown head and back.

Both sexes have yellow underparts and black wings with white bars. The tail is black with white undertail coverts and rump. In winter adults become gray-brown above and below.

Feeding wherever weeds provide seeds, this gregarious species is heard twittering on waste ground, roadsides, gardens and especially weed-filled fields.

Pine Siskin: heavily streaked above and below. **Tanagers:** larger; males have red heads, females olive-green heads. **Yellow-colored Warblers:** slim bills for insect eating. **Evening Grosbeak:** larger with even heavier bill. **Orioles:** much larger.

CHIPPING SPARROW
INTERNAL MIGRANT 5¼in

Plain gray breast; only juveniles' are streaked. Summer: chestnut brown cap with bold white eyebrow stripe. Winter: cap becomes streaked, eyebrow stripe darkens.

Sexes alike. Under the white eyebrow is a black eye stripe that fades in winter. The back plumage is brown streaked with black. Immatures cause confusion by having streaks on breast and crown.

Abundant, this familiar bird is found in woods and fields, and widely from farms to suburbs and towns. The call is "chip" and the song a trill on the same pitch. A summer visitor over most of the area.

Female **Lark Bunting** and **Savannah**, **Song** and **Fox Sparrows**: whitish, streaked breasts. **White-throated**, **White-crowned**, **Field** and **American Tree Sparrows**: striped crowns.

Almost all black, with very long wings and stub tail, producing "rocking" flight.

Body usually described as cigar-shaped, this swallow-type has a squared-off tail with projecting quills.

Nests in chimneys and barns. Seen aloft over towns, sweeping across the sky for insects, giving chittering call on the wing.

White-throated Swift: pied plumage and forked tail. **Purple Martin:** bigger, with forked tail. **Swallows:** very pale or white underparts. **Nightjars:** generally bigger, mostly brown and nocturnal, the **Common Nighthawk** being an exception.

Swallow-types, white below. Tree: entirely blue-green above and widespread. Violet-green: white extends over eye, and outer rump; found only on the west coast.

The juvenile birds are marked similarly but are gray-brown above, the Tree Swallow with a hint of a breast bar which can cause confusion with the Bank Swallow.

Migratory species, they flock together in huge numbers before returning south for the winter. Mainly associated with wooded areas they are also noted as popular garden visitors, where they frequently occupy nest-boxes.

All other Swallow-types have marked or colored underparts.

Prominent white eye stripe. No white on cocked tail.

A large rufous wren, darker above. The tail and wings are barred, but the back is not.

An eastern species, this wren is common around any area providing good ground cover, whether marshes, woodland or overgrown suburban gardens. As with other wrens, has a disproportionately powerful clear song.

House Wren: lacks prominent eye stripe, back and belly bars.
Bewick's Wren: white eye stripe, white on outer tail.

Able to move about on tree trunks in any direction.
Unstreaked white underparts.

White-faced, with a blue-gray back and wings, this is the
largest nuthatch. The underparts can show some rufous but
this is sometimes difficult to see, and variable. Male is black-
capped, female is blue-gray capped.

Found in many wooded habitats, this attractive bird is also a
common visitor at feeders. Often associating with chickadees
and kinglets, this stumpy-tailed little bird has a jerky
awkward flight. Eats insects, and nuts — frequently hoarded.

Red-breasted Nuthatch: rufous underparts. White eyebrow
stripe. **Brown Creeper:** ascends tree trunks. Brown-backed,
curved bill. **Black-and-White Warblers:** able to move about
on tree trunks in any direction. Dark streaks on flanks. **Blue-
gray Gnatcatcher;** long black and white tail.

Male has a red forehead and eyebrow band on a brown head and back. Female has softly streaked face and upperparts.

Seed-eating bill. The male has a red breast and rump with a pale belly and streaked flanks. The female also has heavily streaked underparts. The tail is almost blunt.

Very numerous, this is a most successful introduced species, now quite a familiar sight at feeders. Normal habitats include towns, suburbs and farmland.

Purple Finch: male has red head and back. Female has boldly streaked upperparts and a dark jaw stripe. The tail is cleft. **Cardinal** and male **Tanagers:** much larger and much more obviously red without the streaking.

HOUSE SPARROW
RESIDENT 6in

Male: gray crown, chestnut nape and black bib. Female: unmarked gray-brown crown, and a pale eye stripe.

Male has a brown back streaked with black, very pale gray cheeks and underparts, a gray rump and a white wing bar. The female's back is duller than the male but is also streaked.

Well-known for its tameness in towns, but also common on farmland, often in flocks and in association with other species. Sparrows, like finches, have deep bills typical of birds that eat grain.

Male: none. Female: immature **White-crowned Sparrow**: crown stripe. **Chipping Sparrow**: summer adult has white eye stripe; winter adult has streaked crown. **American Tree Sparrow**: adults have rufous crown, gray eye stripe. **Field Sparrow**: gray eye stripe and marked crown.

Species illustrated: **Oregon** (left), **Slate-colored** (right)

White outer tail feathers and belly. Male: head and breast varied gray shades. Female: head and breast gray-brown.

Previously considered as 6 species. "Slate-colored" and "White-winged" have upperparts the same color as the head. "Oregon," "Pink-sided," "Gray-headed" and "Red-backed" have rufous backs in contrast. All adults are unstreaked.

Found across nearly all of North America, this variable species favors many habitats, notably woodland, brush, dense undergrowth, and suburban feeders.

Rufous-sided Towhee: heavy dark bill, rufous sides.

Whitish, streaked breast. Long rounded tail. Has both crown and eyebrow stripes which vary in color.

The eye and crown stripes can be white or gray. The brown upperparts are streaked, as are the pale underparts. Whitish throat. The breast streaks often form a marked central spot, but this may be hard to see. The belly is whitish.

A common sparrow of brush areas, it is often seen at roadsides and in gardens. It particularly favors thickets near water. The form pictured above is typical of several subspecies which vary across its range.

Savannah Sparrow: whitish, streaked breast. Short cleft tail. Juvenile **American Tree, White-throated** and **White-crowned Sparrows:** streaked gray or buff breasts. Adult **Field, Chipping, American Tree, White-throated** and **White-crowned Sps:** plain breasts. **Fox Sp.:** no crown stripe.

Plain gray above with a prominent crest.

Black forehead. White underparts and mask. Rusty flanks.

Common in their original woodland habitat, and also in parks and suburban gardens, frequently at feeders.

Cedar Waxwing: brown above, yellow tip to tail. **Carolina** and **Black-capped Chickadee:** black cap and bib. **Bushtits** and **Nuthatches:** lack crest.

25

DOWNY WOODPECKER
RESIDENT **6½in**

♂

White-backed, short-billed.

Small for a woodpecker. Pied plumage, all white below, white outer tail feathers, eyebrow, mustache, and spots on the wings. The male shows a red nape patch.

Numerous in forests, woods, orchards, parks, and at garden feeders. The bill is used both to chisel out nest holes and to get at its insect prey.

Other **Woodpeckers** and **Sapsuckers** lack white backs, short bills or are larger, note particularly the **Hairy Woodpecker**.

Flycatching behavior. Has no wing bars or eye rings. Tail is all gray-brown.

Gray-brown above. Pale below although breast may be partially shaded.

Insect-eaters, they leave a favorite perch, catch their prey and return. The tail is repeatedly pumped. Found in habitats ranging from woodland to farmland and suburbs.

Empidonax Flycatchers: have two wing bars and eye rings, **Willow:** only lacking eye rings. **Eastern and Western Wood-Pewees:** two wing bars but no eye rings. **Kingbirds:** lack eye rings. White on tail.

CEDAR WAXWING
INTERNAL MIGRANT **7in**

Yellow-tipped tail, and pale yellow belly.

Brown above, the tail is pale gray becoming dark before the tip. Undertail coverts are white. The wings are dark gray with remarkable red "wax" tips on secondaries. Juveniles are streaked below.

Gregarious, flocks of waxwings feed on berries and insects in woodland and orchards. Should they overfeed, they can sometimes barely fly.

None.

Male: glossy blue-black body, brown head. Female: gray-brown, paler below, in association with male.

Young birds resemble a streaked female underneath. Young males develop patchy intermediate markings before acquiring full adult plumage.

As well as woodland, often found in association with farm buildings, parkland and suburbs. Gregarious, frequently in mixed flocks, the cowbirds are smaller than other blackbirds, feeding with tails lifted.

Brewer's Blackbird: male is yellow-eyed, purple-headed. Female is uniform above and below. **Purple Martin:** male is entirely blue-black. **Common Grackle:** far larger, remarkable keel-shaped tail. **Starling:** spangled plumage.

PURPLE MARTIN
SUMMER VISITOR **8in**

Swallow-type, glossy purple above and (male) below.

The largest swallow-type. Females and juveniles are gray below. The tail is forked.

A migratory species. They fly with quick wing beats and glide easily in pursuit of insects. Found anywhere in association with buildings, readily using Martin houses. Loud, rich call.

Barn Swallow: very forked tail and red face. **Tree Swallow:** small, adult blue-green above and white below. **Starling:** confusion only in flight. Spangled plumage, square tail.

Massive bill. White patches on trailing inner wing.

Black wings and tail, yellow on inner underwing. The body of the male is brown and yellow with a prominent yellow forehead. The female has a gray and buff body with touches of yellow reminiscent of the male.

A woodland species, it does frequent feeders in winter. Gregarious, often located by penetrating "clee-ip" and "cleeer" calls.

American Goldfinch and winter **Snow Bunting**: smaller, with smaller short bill. **Rose-breasted** and **Black-headed Grosbeak:** massive bills, white on forewing. Female **Orioles:** sharp bills.

NORTHERN ORIOLE
SUMMER VISITOR **8½in**

♀

♂

♂

♀

Male: long black tail with orange outer tail feathers.
Female: similar to male with duller orange-yellow breast.

Both "Baltimore" and "Bullock's" subspecies have the male
with orange rump and underparts, black back and wings.
"Bullock's" has orange on face, more white in wings. The
female resembles male but is mostly olive-brown above.

Both subspecies favor wooded areas and suburbs. The
"Baltimore" is the northern and eastern representative, and
the "Bullock's" inhabits the southern and western areas.
There is some overlap.

Male **Black-headed Grosbeak**: massive bill, black tail.
American Robin, Yellow-headed Blackbird: dark brown or
black tail.

EASTERN KINGBIRD

8½in SUMMER VISITOR

Flycatching behavior. White band at tip of tail.

Upperparts slate-gray/black. Underparts very white except for grayish area on upper breast. A few orange-red feathers in the crown are sometimes visible. Juveniles brown but resemble adults.

An insect-eater, this bird darts and even hovers in the chase for prey. It then returns to its favorite perch on a stump or branch in a clearing. A noisy familiar bird of the suburbs, often to be seen on telegraph wires.

Other **Kingbirds**, **Flycatchers**, **Pewees** and **Phoebes** share flycatching behavior but lack white band at tip of tail.

EUROPEAN STARLING
RESIDENT 8½in

Spangled body plumage, iridescent in summer, and white-specked in winter.

Plump-bodied with short pointed wings. The wing feathers are brown-edged, visible when the bird is at rest. Juveniles are a uniform mouse-brown, progressing to adult plumage.

A very successful introduced species, it is now abundant in towns, parks, gardens and open farmland. It walks jerkily and flies with a fast direct action, characteristically triangular in flight. Very gregarious, roosts communally.

Purple Martin, Blackbirds, Grackles and **Cowbirds:** only similar in flight, no spangled plumage

Heavy red cone-shaped bill.

Male is strikingly red overall with a black facial area around the bill. Both sexes have the crest. The female and juveniles are generally browner and duller with red areas in the wing and tail.

Non-migratory, found all year round in woodland, swamps and suburbs. Varied song consists of penetrating loud rich whistles, given from prominent perches.

Male **Tanagers** and both **Waxwings** only superficially similar — all lack red bill.

Black cap and tail with chestnut undertail coverts.

Otherwise uniformly gray.

Usually secretive, it remains hidden in undergrowth. Flicks tail. Irritatingly persistent cat-like "mew" call is distinctive.

Juvenile **Gray Jay:** larger, no black cap or tail. **Loggerhead Shrike:** black eye stripe. **Northern Mockingbird:** white wing patches and outer tail feathers.

RED-WINGED BLACKBIRD

8½in RESIDENT/SUMMER V.

Sharp pointed bill. Male: red-shouldered black bird.
Female: very heavily streaked underparts.

The male's red patch is bordered with yellow. The female's
back and streaks below are dark gray-brown giving an
overall brown impression. The immature male resembles the
female but with a red shoulder patch.

This common species nests in marshes and fields and forages
in more fruitful surrounding areas. The birds are aggressive
but form enormous winter flocks.

Female **House** and **Purple Finch**: stubby seed-eating bill.
Pine Siskin: much smaller, prominent yellow flight feathers.

RED-HEADED WOODPECKER

RESIDENT/SUMMER V. **9in**

Prominent white inner wing patches. Adult: the entire head is red. White underparts.

The remainder of the adults' plumage is black. The juvenile is mostly barred brown above and is streaked below. All ages share a white rump which connects the wing patches.

Fairly numerous, this typical woodpecker has the supportive stiff tail and two backward-facing toes for climbing. A varied diet of insects and fruit and acorns which are stored for winter. Favors woods, farms and orchards.

All other **Woodpeckers** and **Sapsuckers:** adults show only partial red coloration of the head, if any. Immatures lack the prominent white wing patches.

Long pointed wings with white bars. Active during the day as well as at night.

Gray-brown mottled plumage above provides remarkably effective camouflage on the ground or on a branch. Breast, belly and tail are barred. Both sexes have throat marks, white in the male, buff in the female.

Called "goatsuckers," they have a large gape for catching insects on the wing. In legend this gape was for sucking milk from goats. Silent and masterful fliers, they are to be seen in open woodland or in towns, often nesting on flat roofs

Whip-poor-will: rounded wings. Mostly nocturnal. **Swifts**: day feeders, no brown plumage. **Kestrels, Cuckoos**: lack white bars on wings.

Large area of white on the wings and white outer tail feathers, especially prominent in flight.

Gray above, paler below. Brown-black tail and wings, apart from white areas mentioned above.

Noted for their prolonged repetitious song, often mimicking other species and even sundry interesting noises. Seen about suburbs and farms, also in thickets. A wing-flashing display is given during courtship and territorial defense.

Loggerhead Shrike: does have a small wing patch, but also a prominent black mask. **Gray Catbird:** no white markings, black crown. **Gray Jay:** no white wing patches, black nape.

Gray back and brick-red breast. No wing bars.

The female's back is a little browner and the breast a little less red. The juvenile's breast is spotted. All have whitish undertail coverts. The adults' throats are white streaked with black.

Originally a woodland species, it is now a very familiar sight on lawns and in parks. It feeds on worms, insects and, notably, berries.

Varied Thrushes: Wing bars. Other **Thrushes** with spotted breasts lack brick-red coloration.

Deep-chested chicken-shaped birds. California Quail: teardrop shaped plume. Northern Bobwhite: pale throat and eye stripes. Crested.

Males are beautifully marked with females similar but duller and browner. Both species are short-tailed and round-winged giving a rapid take-off and flight action.

The California Quail is found only in the west in open woodland, open country and suburbs. The Northern Bobwhite is an eastern species of open woodland and farmland. Both feed on seeds, insects and berries.

Ruffed and **Sharp-tailed Grouse:** much larger with longer tails. **Sora:** water-bird without crest or plume.

Two prominent black breast bands.

Brown crown, ear coverts and back with orange-brown rump. White underparts, wing bar and outer tail feathers. The tail is long and diamond-shaped.

Common in farm fields, parkland, lawns, airports and river banks. This species feeds on insects and worms and is familiar from coast to coast. The noisy call "kill-deeeah" gives rise to its name. Feigns injury when in danger.

None.

Blue crest. Blue tail edged with white.

Predominantly blue above and whitish below, the wings are barred with black and white. The black necklace extends around behind the face.

Noisy, often screaming "jay, jay," and very visible in gardens and woodland alike.

Steller's Jay: blue crest. Tail all blue. **Gray** and **Scrub Jays:** lack crest. **Bluebird:** smaller, no crest.

Serrated and tapering diamond-shaped tail.

Brown above and pinkish below. There is a black neck spot, also black spots on the back and inner wing. The outer wing is blue-gray. The tail is edged with white.

It derives its name from the mournful cooing call. Normally found commonly in and around towns and suburbs, it is also widely present near farms, scrub and grasslands. The wings produce a whistle as the bird takes off.

Cuckoos: very long slender tails. **Black-billed Magpie:** blackish diamond-shaped tail not tapered or serrated.

Remarkable keel-shaped tail.

Apparently all black with yellow eyes, the male is actually glossy purple (a "bronze" form shows browner back and flanks), whilst the female and juveniles are duller. The juvenile has brown eyes.

Common. Usually gregarious in fields, parks and suburbs.

Cowbirds: smaller, normal tails. **Brewer's Blackbird:** smaller, normal tail. **Starling:** spangled plumage, short tail.

Familiar pigeon of the city with a "cooo-cuk-cuk-cooo" call.

Plumage very variable. Those most like wild ancestors are gray with a white rump and two large black wing bars. Other common varieties are black, brown, white or mottled gray, often without the white rump. Wings are long and pointed.

May form large flocks in towns and on farmland where damage to crops may result. Their large messy nests are a common sight on buildings and bridges. Town variants are probably derived from domesticated wild Rock Doves.

Mourning Dove: serrated and tapering diamond-shaped tail — can be short in juvenile. **Prairie Falcon:** fast direct flier, similar profile, but only mistaken briefly in flight.

Brown barred back, round-spotted underparts. ("Yellow-shafted" form: golden-yellow underwing. "Red-shafted" form: red underwing.)

Black crescent-shaped bib, and black tail. The white rump is prominent in flight. Male birds have a mustache and both sexes of the "Yellow" form have red nape patches. The "Red" form lacks this.

Extremely undulating in flight, the rump and underwing are both normally visible. On the ground flickers hop in search of ants. On trees the stiff tail feathers provide support. A common species in woodland and suburbs. Loud ringing call.

Yellow-bellied Sapsucker: juveniles barred beneath.

Entirely black with "caw" call note.

Juvenile's call note is a nasal "cah," mainly restricted to begging.

Widespread, this species is common and gregarious around many habitats, especially cultivated fields, woodland and river margins.

Common Raven: much larger, "pruk" call note.

Very large "eared" owl with heavily barred underparts.

Rusty colored face with yellow eyes. White-throated. Back and tail are mottled grayish-buff and dark brown.

Inhabits woodlands, forests, open country, caves, and also towns. Predominantly nocturnal. Large enough to take even sizeable mammals and birds

Other "eared" **Owls** all small, other large **Owls** lack "ears."

Tiny bird with colorful crown edged black.

Both sexes have a white eyebrow stripe, a black eye stripe, and two prominent white wing bars. The upperparts are olive-green, paler below. The male's crown is red edged with yellow. The female's is yellow.

Widespread and common, these tiny birds flit about coniferous forests and mixed woodland. Their thin "see-see-see" notes are usually the first indication of their presence.

Ruby-crowned Kinglet: tiny, bold white eye ring broken above eye. **Red-eyed Vireo:** similar pattern of eye stripes, plain crown, no wing bars. Some smaller **Warblers** may be confused in foliage, but all are larger with a slimmer profile. **Blue-gray Gnatcatcher:** long black and white tail.

Hummingbird with rufous-red in the tail.

Green crown and wings, rufous flanks and white underparts. The male is rufous-backed and red-throated. The female has a spotted throat. Back and central tail are green. The female also has black and white tail edgings.

Found only in the northwest, this typical hummingbird drinks nectar from flowers through its specially adapted bill. In display, the male describes a vertical oval flight. Common in thickets, woodland edges.

Ruby-throated Hummingbird: only hummingbird seen in the east. Greenish or buff flanks. **Black-chinned Hummingbirds:** greenish flanks.

Tiny bird with bold white eye ring broken above the eye.

Both sexes have two prominent white wing bars. The upperparts are olive-green, paler below. The male may show a red crown patch, but it is rarely seen, and the female lacks it completely.

Widespread and common, these tiny birds flit about coniferous forests and mixed woodland. Their "tsee" and similar notes are usually the first indication of their presence.

Golden-crowned Kinglet: tiny, colorful crown edged black. **Solitary Vireo:** white "spectacles" and plain crown. Beware, some small **Warblers** have eye rings and may be confused in foliage, but all are larger with a slimmer profile. **Blue-gray Gnatcatcher:** long black and white tail.

♂

Heavily streaked above and below. Black wings show yellow in flight.

Thin seed-eating bill. Brown upperparts, paler below. Tail is black and cleft with yellow markings at base.

Numerous in coniferous and mixed woodland, this species is also found in fields and on weeds with seed heads.

American Goldfinch: unstreaked body, black wings. Female **House Finch:** lacks yellow markings. **Evening Grosbeak:** much larger, massive bill, white patches on trailing inner wing.

Plain olive above (no wing bars) contrasting with very yellow throat. Male has a heavy black mask in addition.

The belly is whitish, as is the upper border of the male's mask.

A very common bird in its habitat of swamps, wet thickets and lush fields, it is secretive and often located by its clear song "witchety, witchety, witchety, witch." It is a summer visitor over most of North America.

Wilson's Warbler: back is plain olive, yellow forehead. Other similar **Warblers** have wing bars. Winter **American Goldfinch:** wings are black. **Redstarts** and **Flycatchers** lack very yellow throat.

Tree-ascending behavior and downward-curved bill.

Small, active, mouse-like bird. Brown above with white underparts and eye stripe. Buff wing bars.

Aptly named, normally seen spiraling tree trunks in search of insects. The stiff tail feathers are used for support like a woodpecker. Primarily a forest and woodland bird, it may visit gardens.

Carolina and **Bewick's Wrens:** have curved bills, but not the ascending behavior. **Nuthatches:** climb over trees in all directions, have straight bills and are blue-gray above.

Bright patches of color (male - orange, female - yellow) on wings and upper outer tail feathers.

Male is glossy black above and on the breast. Female is olive above with a grayer head. Both sexes have white undertail coverts, and the inverted T on the tail is distinctive.

An active flycatching species, it flits after its prey in woodlands, where it is numerous. It has a habit of displaying its spread tail and wings at a favorite perch, showing the bright coloration to the full.

Male **Northern Oriole**: larger, and orange is on lower outer tail.

Whitish, streaked breast. Short cleft tail. Pale crown and eyebrow stripes, the latter usually yellowish.

The brown upperparts are streaked, as are the pale underparts. The belly and undertail are normally white.

A bird of open country, this species frequents grassland, fresh and salt marshes, dunes and prairies. Abundant. There are subspecies across its range, all similar to the figure above.

Song Sparrow: whitish, streaked breast. Long tail. Juvenile **Chipping, American Tree, White-crowned** and **White-throated Sparrows:** streaked gray or buff breasts. **House** and adult **Field, Chipping, American Tree, White-crowned** and **White-throated Sparrows:** plain breasts.

Species illustrated is Least Flycatcher.

Flycatching behavior. All have two wing bars and a pale eye ring, except Willow Flycatcher which lacks eye ring but shows olive green back.

The Least, Acadian, Alder, Buff-breasted, Dusky, Gray, Hammond's, Western, Willow and Yellow-bellied Flycatchers are all varying olive-green tones above, paler below, often with a yellow tinge.

Variously found in woodland, farmland and wet habitats, they are best separated from each other by locality and voice, but may be taken together until expert. Insect-eaters, they have a favorite perch, catch their prey, and return.

Eastern and Western Wood-Pewees: have two wing bars but no eye rings. Gray-brown above. **Eastern Phoebe:** lacks wing bars and eye rings. **Kingbirds:** lack eye rings, show white on tail.

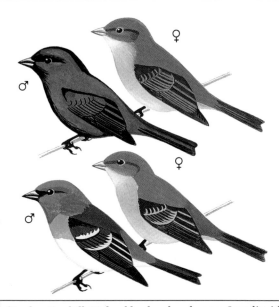

Seed-eating bill. Males: blue head and rump, Lazuli with two prominent wing bars. Females: unusually plain, Indigo with breast streaks, Lazuli two faint wing bars.

Indigo males are blue all over but can molt to closely resemble female. Lazuli males have a pale belly with a cinnamon breast and sides. Hybrids may be produced where the two species overlap ranges and interbreed.

Summer visitors, they frequent open wooded areas and bush. The Lazuli particularly prefer stream areas.

Bluebirds: males light blue above, and all have the slim bill of an insect-eater. No wing bars. Female House Sparrow: eye-striped. Female Brown-headed Cowbird: larger and grayer. Winter American Goldfinch: black-winged, whitish rump.

Yellow-rumped with yellow side patch and crown patch.

Appears black and white except for patches of yellow. The western "Audubon's" form additionally has a yellow throat patch. The belly is white with streaks, the upperparts are gray tones with streaks.

A very common bird in its normal habitat of forests and woods, it is widespread although migratory within the North American continent. In winter it is also seen in brush and thickets.

Female **American Redstart**: yellow on wing and outer tail. **Black-and-White, Black-throated Green Warblers**: lack these yellow patches. Any other similar **Warblers** are quite uncommon and all lack this combination of yellow marks.

SOLITARY VIREO
INTERNAL MIGRANT **5½in**

Bold white eye ring and loral stripe form "spectacles."
Sturdy bill is curved and hooked.

There is east-to-west color variation: eastern birds are gray-
headed, green-backed, two yellow wing bars, yellow flanks.
The Rockies form is gray with two white wing bars. The
western form is green above, yellow-flanked with white bars.

Abundant in mixed woodlands, high in foliage, and feeds in a
deliberate unobtrusive fashion. This and the stockier build
saves confusion with warblers, and the lower posture and no
flycatching behavior saves confusion with flycatchers.

White-eyed Vireo: yellow "spectacles." **Red-eyed** and
Warbling Vireos: have eyebrow stripes but no "spectacles."
Warblers: have straight delicate bills and no "spectacles."

Sturdy bill is curved and hooked. The prominent white eyebrow stripe is edged black above and below.

Gray cap, olive back and pale underparts. The red eye is rarely seen, only at very close range. Sometimes flanks are yellowish.

A woodland species, it is very common in the east, but almost absent in the west. The song is a monotonous "chway," often sung all day in bursts.

Solitary and **White-eyed Vireos:** white and yellow "spectacles" respectively. **Warbling Vireo:** bold white eyebrow stripe, with faint dark eye stripe. **Warblers:** straight, delicate bills, very active feeders.

Flycatching behavior. Two wing bars but no eye rings. Gray-brown above. Eastern, Western: east and west respectively of the 100th meridian.

Gray-brown above, but does vary. Paler below although breast is shaded darker. Adult has black upper bill, orange lower bill.

Name is derived from "pee-a-wee" and similar calls. Insect-eaters, they leave a favorite perch, catch their prey, and return. Normally found in forests, woodlands and suburban trees.

The following share flycatching behavior: **Empidonax Flycatchers:** all have two wing bars and eye rings, **Willow** excepted — no eye ring, olive-green above. **Eastern Phoebe:** lacks wing bars and eye rings. **Kingbirds:** lack eye rings, white on tail.

♂ ●

Very white-winged for a small bird.

Winter plumage only really applies, with both sexes white below, around the face and on the outer tail feathers. The back is heavily streaked, the crown and rump orange-brown. Wing tips and central tail feathers are black.

Breeds in summer on the northern tundra, but in winter is widely found in fields, shores, roadsides and increasingly at feeders.

Grosbeaks: bigger birds, but white patches in wings smaller, and body colors very different.

BARN SWALLOW
SUMMER VISITOR **7in**

Long forked tail and red face.

Blue-black back and buff below. Blue band at throat and blue cheeks border the red face. The tail feathers have white spots above and patches below.

An acrobatic flier, catching insects on the wing at speed, often at very low level. Frequently nests inside farm buildings. A summer visitor, it is seen to gather on telegraph wires before returning south.

Purple Martin: blue-black above, including face, cleft tail. **Tree/Violet-green Swallows:** white underparts, cleft tail. **Bank Swallow:** brown breast bar, cleft tail. **Cliff Swallow:** buff rump, square tail.

W ♂   E ♂   ♀

Blue above with a red breast. Eastern: red extends up side of neck and throat. Western: red ceases above the breast.

The flanks are also red, the belly and undertail whitish. The females are duller than the males with grayish heads, and the juveniles have speckled breasts, although they still show bright blue on the wings.

Frequents woodland, orchards, farmlands and open country with some trees. Populations have declined over the years, apparently due to competition for nest-holes with more dominant species.

Mountain Bluebird: similar above, no red breast. **Blue** and **Steller's Jay:** much larger, no red breast. Male **Lazuli Bunting:** turquoise above with two white wing bars.

67

WHITE-CROWNED SPARROW
INTERNAL MIGRANT **7in**

Plain gray throat and breast, only the juvenile being streaked. Dark cap has eyebrow and crown stripes.

Sexes alike. The back is brown streaked with black but the rump and tail are plain. The bill is pink. Immatures are brown-capped and the stripes are buff. Juveniles streaked above and below. Small variations among subspecies.

Numerous, this migratory sparrow is mostly seen as a winter visitor as it breeds in the northern tundra and the Rockies. Seen in woodlands, parks and at roadsides, it is increasingly reported at feeders.

White-throated Sparrow: white throat, yellow before eyes. **Chipping** and female **House Sparrows:** brown crown, unstriped. **Field** and **American Tree Sparrows:** light crowns, striped. **Savannah, Song** and **Fox Sparrows:** whitish, streaked breasts.

Thick-billed. Male: bright red head, black wings and tail. Female: olive-colored above, olive-yellow below.

Scarlet Tanager: Male is otherwise bright red, female has an unstreaked crown. No wing bars. Western Tanager: male is otherwise yellow, female has streaked crown. Both sexes have two clear wing bars. Males molt to green in winter.

Forest and woodland species, both are common summer visitors. They eat insects and fruit. The bill is fairly heavy and is notched.

Summer T.: red-winged male, fem. muddy yellow below. **North. Oriole:** fem. gray-brown above, pale orange below. **Cardinal:** red wings, cone-shaped bill. **Red-head W'pecker:** white on wings. Fem. **Am. Goldfinch:** smaller stubby bill. **Flycatchers, Warblers, Vireos** like females: lack thick bill.

HORNED LARK
INTERNAL MIGRANT **7½in**

Black "horns" and cheek pattern.

Some variation, but basically brown, streaked underparts, a pale face, a black upper breast band, and softly streaked underparts, often with a noticeable buff tinge. From below undertail is dark brown with white outer tail markings.

Numerous and widespread, this pleasing songster is usually seen in the air above fields, prairies, tundra, shores and airports. On the ground they are camouflaged. They walk, not hop. Main food is insects and seeds.

Eastern/Western Meadowlark: much larger, lack "horns," V-shaped breast band. **Sparrows, Warblers:** all lack "horns."

RUFOUS-SIDED TOWHEE

8in INTERNAL MIGRANT

W ♂

E ♂
♀

Heavy dark bill, rufous sides.

Both sexes have white underparts, wing patches and a white-cornered tail. The male is otherwise black, the female brown. Juveniles are brown, streaked above and below. Western "spotted" forms have white spots on the back.

A ground feeder, common in open woodland, thickets and dense undergrowth. The song of eastern birds is usually written as "drink-your-tea-ee."

Black-headed and **Rose-breasted Grosbeak:** massive pale bills, white on forewings. Female **Dark-eyed Junco:** white outer tail feathers.

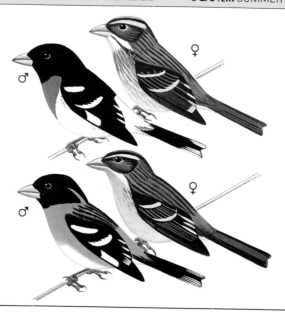

Massive pale bill. White on forewings. Males: black-headed. Females: bold eyebrow stripe.

Rose-breasted male has red breast and inner wing, white rump and underparts, mostly black above. Female brown above, streaked pale below. Black-headed male has orange breast, rump, mostly black above. Female, yellowish below.

Both species are common. The Rose-breasted is found in rather scrubby habitat, whilst the Black-headed favors woodland edges. Summer visitors, with similar melodic robin-like songs.

Rufous-sided Towhee: male, black-headed, heavy dark bill; female, unmarked brown head. **Evening Grosbeak:** massive pale bill. White patches on trailing inner wing. **Sparrows** and other species similar to the female lack the massive bill.

The white wing patch is in the forewing. Adults show yellow belly.

Adults have red forehead, black upper breast and upperparts, except for white stripes on head, bars on back and tail, and a white rump. The male's throat is red, the female's white. Immatures are brown, but share wing patches.

Widespread and common in forests and wooded areas, sapsuckers drill neat rows of holes in trees to obtain the sap. Highly migratory within the North American continent.

Downy and **Hairy Woodpeckers:** no white wing patch, but back is white. **Northern Flicker:** no white wing patch. **Red-headed Woodpecker:** white wing patch on rear inner wing.

Black and gray plumage with an obvious black mask.

Black wings show a white wing patch and the black tail is white-edged. Upperparts are gray and underparts whitish.

"Butcher-birds," shrikes descend on their prey from a perch, frequently impaling the victim on a thorn to form a "larder," often forgotten. Found in open country and scrubland.

Northern Mockingbird and **Gray Jay**: lack black mask.

E

Black V on the yellow breast.

The upperparts are brown with black streaks on the head and upper back, becoming black bars on down to the tail. Outer tail feathers are notably white. The yellow extends to the belly but the flanks are whitish and streaked. Sharp bill.

Common, these species together are found across the United States, the Eastern bird being darker and more distinctively marked. They frequent fields, meadows and prairies, flying short distances in bursts before settling again.

Horned Lark: much smaller, black "horns" and cheek pattern.

A small, low-flying round-winged bird of prey.

Gray crown, back and upper wings. The underparts are barred rusty red, the undertail coverts are white and the square tail is barred. Immature birds are brown above, very pale below, streaked, not barred, with black.

A woodland hawk, it flies with quick wingbeats interspersed with glides, and then drops onto its prey, usually small birds or mammals. Widespread in woodland areas, it is a partial migrant.

Red-tailed, **Red-shouldered** and **Broad-winged Hawks**: all markedly larger soaring hawks. **American Kestrel**: also small but hovers. Pointed wings. **Eagles** and **Vultures**: huge by comparison.

Small for a bird of prey, a falcon, it hovers repeatedly.

Rufous back and tail. Underparts pale and streaked. The white cheeks have two black stripes. A black band at the tail tip is seen when hovering. Male has blue-gray wings above. Both sexes have dark bars across back, female also on the tail.

Falcons have pointed wings, clearly visible in this species. Often seen hovering or perched on favorite posts with an upright posture, this is our commonest falcon, found widely in open country and in towns.

Sharp-shinned Hawk: also small but does not hover. Rounded wings. Other birds of prey are larger and do not hover.

BROWN THRASHER
INTERNAL MIGRANT **11½in**

Disproportionately long rufous tail.

Rufous brown above with two white wing bars. Long bill. Streaked pattern of spots on otherwise whitish underparts.

Found almost exclusively east of the Rockies, this species is commonplace along hedgerows, in thickets and brush. A notable songbird related to mockingbirds and catbirds.

Northern Mockingbird: same profile, but grayer with white wing patches. **Thrushes** and **Robins** are brown above with spots below, but tails and bills are medium length only, and all in proportion.

White forehead and black nape patch.

Gray overall, paler below. White collar and cheeks. Fluffy. Juveniles are a sooty gray all over.

Numerous in coniferous forests, bold and visible.

Northern Mockingbird: gray-headed with large white areas on wings. **Loggerhead Shrike:** gray-headed, black mask. **Gray Catbird:** black cap.

YELLOW-BILLED CUCKOO
SUMMER VISITOR **12in**

Yellow lower bill and rufous wing patch.

Gray-brown above, white below. The extremely long tail is black, with bold white spots. The bill is downcurved.

A summer visitor, common enough around woodland, orchards and thickets.

Black-billed Cuckoo: black-billed, no rufous wing patch.
Mourning Dove, Black-billed Magpie: have long tails but are otherwise dissimilar.

RUFFED GROUSE

17½in RESIDENT

Medium length fan-shaped tail.

Typical game-bird with chicken shape. Crested, brown above, paler and barred below. The tail has a white-edged black band at the tip, very prominent in all plumages, especially when fanned. Note the male's dark gray ruff.

A woodland bird, usually seen exploding noisily from cover, or heard giving a "thumping" display call during courtship. At this time the male erects the crest and ruff, and fans the tail.

Female **California Quail** and **Nothern Bobwhite:** far smaller, short tails. Female **Ring-necked Pheasant** and **Sharp-tailed Grouse:** tapered tails. **Wild Turkey:** far larger, bare head.

Pied plumage with exceptionally long wedge-ended tail.

Black bill. Black plumage is actually dark blue and dark green in parts. Otherwise black except for white on belly, wing tips and shoulders.

An unmistakable member of the crow family, found in open woods, scrub and open range. It will eat almost anything, but is a notorious thief of the eggs of smaller birds.

Mourning Dove and **Yellow-billed Cuckoo** have long tails but are otherwise dissimilar.

A soaring hawk. When seen in flight from below, shows a
thin but distinct dark leading edge to the inner underwing.

Plumage variable. "Red-tail" relates to upper tail of adults.
Head, back, wings are dark brown above. Pale below, belly is
streaked. "Fingertips" are dark. "Kruider's" Grt. Plains pale
form contrasts with "Harlan's" (Canada/Alaska) dark form.

Feeds on rodents, reptiles and rabbits over its wide range.
This common hawk can be seen in diverse habitats:
woodland, groves, prairies and desert. It has a distinctive
call-note, a harsh descending "keeeer."

Vultures, Eagles: much larger. **Harriers,** "Woodland"
Hawks: low fliers. **Falcons:** pointed wings. **Red-shouldered,
Broad-winged Hawks:** also soaring hawks but have a very
broad dark leading edge to the inner underwing.

COMMON RAVEN
RESIDENT 25in

Entirely black, "pruk" call-note.

In flight the wedge-shaped tail is distinctive. At rest, the heavy bill and shaggy throat feathers also provide good features for identification.

Favors mountainous cliffs, but also forests and deserts. Widespread and reasonably common, it is a masterful flier, unexpectedly acrobatic during courtship. At other times it is a stately soaring flier, flapping its wings periodically.

American Crow: smaller; "caw" call-note.

Underwing pattern in flight entirely black except for clearly defined whitish "fingers" at the end of the primaries. Naked head.

Head is gray. Remainder of plumage is black. The gray legs may protrude beyond the tail in flight.

The wings are broad, the tail short, and flight seems a labored action. This species inhabits open country but is also common at garbage dumps as an efficient scavenger. Gregarious, roosts communally.

Turkey Vulture: underwing has forewing only dark brown. Remainder is pale gray. **Bald** and **Golden Eagles:** lack defined whitish "fingers" on underwing.

TURKEY VULTURE
RESIDENT/SUMMER V. **28in**

Underwing pattern in flight: forewing is blackish, remainder is pale gray. Head is naked.

Head is red, gray in immatures. Remainder of plumage is dark gray-brown.

Usually seen soaring with a V-shaped wing attitude, they often rock unsteadily in flight. This species is located widely over farmland and any dry areas. Scavengers, not predators, they feed mainly on carrion. May roost communally.

Black Vulture: underwing entirely dark brown except for whitish "fingers" at end of primaries. Naked head. **Bald** and **Golden Eagles:** lack extensive pale gray underwing areas.

SANDHILL CRANE

42in INTERNAL MIGRANT

Untidy "bustle" at rear overhangs the tail feathers.

A gray bird with dark legs and bill, the gray plumage may become brown-stained through preening with a muddied bill. Adults have bare red skin across the crown. The cheeks and chin are white. Immatures are predominantly brown.

Although clearly associated with water, this species spends much of its time feeding in quite dry fields, and is likely to be seen in that habitat. They are noted for a noisy trumpeting call and high altitude flight.

Herons and **Egrets** are also long-legged, but lack the untidy "bustle."

SPOTTED SANDPIPER
INTERNAL MIGRANT **7½in**

Wading bird with medium length bill: (summer) breast
and belly heavily marked with round spots, (winter)
"saddle" mark above shoulders.

Olive-brown plumage above, white below. When breeding,
adults have barred upperparts. A white wing stripe is visible
in flight, as are black and white outer tail feathers. Black eye
stripe with white above.

A common sandpiper of inland waterways, it has a
distinctive stuttering flight on stiff wings. On the ground,
bobs and teeters uncertainly.

(Summer): **Thrushes:** swamp or woodland habitat. Other
waders: spots not round and rarely on belly.
(Winter): **Semipalmated** and other **Plovers:** stubby bill.

Remarkable scuttling run at water's edge, back and forth with the waves.

Usually seen in its pale winter plumage. Light gray above and white below, it shows a prominent white wing stripe, a white eye stripe, with black legs and bill. In summer the whole front half becomes uniform.

In summer it breeds on the Arctic tundra. In the winter we see it on sandy beaches all around our shorelines, feeding in between the waves. This high activity and palest of plumages makes the species distinctive.

No other shorebirds feed running with the waves, but note: **Spotted, Least** and **Pectoral Sandpipers** and **Willet:** have paler colored legs. **Dunlin:** (winter) dark back, (summer) black-bellied. **Semipalmated Sandpiper:** tiny, poorly-defined wing stripe.

Adults are black-bodied.

Wings and cleft tail are all gray, the undertail coverts are white, the bill is black and the short legs are blood-red. First summer immatures are blotchily black on the body, as are molting adults later in the summer — also distinctive.

A summer visitor from S. America, this species is typical of terns, being a buoyant bounding flier with pointed wings, checking to plunge-dive for prey. It feeds at lakes and marshes, sometimes far inland. It mostly migrates coastally.

Other **Terns:** share build and pointed wings, but have pale gray or white bodies. **Gulls:** heavier build and pale bodies.

BELTED KINGFISHER

13in INTERNAL MIGRANT

♀

♂

A typical kingfisher plunging for fish, with blue-gray back and white belly.

Blue-gray crested head, breast bar, wings and tail. The female additionally has a rust-colored belly and flank bar. Note the dagger-like bill.

This is the only common American kingfisher and is found along streams, lakes, estuaries and coasts. It nests in holes in banks. Often seen apparently out of habitat on telegraph wires.

Jays: do not plunge for fish.

BONAPARTE'S GULL
INTERNAL MIGRANT **13in**

The upperwing is pale gray with a white wedge at the tip.

Small gulls. The back is pale gray, the bill black and the legs red. In summer they are black-headed, but this diminishes to an "ear spot" in winter. Immatures show brown in wings and a black tail-tip, emphasizing the blunt tail.

This coastal species is seen inland infrequently, except around the Great Lakes. Small enough to be confused with a tern, it is a buoyant bounding flier with quick wingbeats.

Other **Gulls** are substantially larger and lack the wedge of white at the wing tip. **Terns** have cleft or forked tails.

Stocky profile with abrupt tail. Summer: deep pale bill encircled by a black ring. Winter: deep unmarked pale bill.

Summer: brown overall with black chin and pale belly. Winter: chin turns white, otherwise more rufous, especially neck. Juveniles are downy and heavily streaked.

Numerous on ponds, marshes and lakes, but not easily seen due to secretive nature. It has the ability to sink to leave only the head above water. Winters on salt water, coastal bays included.

All **Ducks** have flattened bills and pointed tails.

COMMON TERN
SUMMER VISITOR **14in**

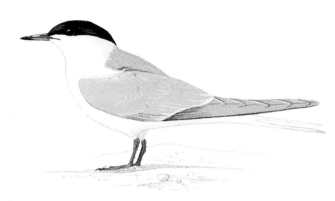

Black cap and nape. Deeply forked tail.

Red bill with black tip. Gray above and white below with a darker area in the wing near the tip. Red feet. Immatures and winter adults show a black bill.

Exclusively associated with water they feed by plunge-diving for fish. Flight is buoyant and bounding. A summer visitor, this is a common species and can be found breeding in huge colonies.

Caspian Tern: much larger, stocky tern. Tail slightly forked. **Black Skimmer:** remarkable bill, lower mandible larger than upper. Tail slightly forked. **Gulls** lack the deeply forked tail. **Black Tern:** black-bodied.

White flank stripe.

Though often appearing black, the back plumage is dark brown. The yellow-tipped red bill and shield are very distinctive, as are the white outer undertail coverts.

Favors a variety of freshwater habitats from marshes and small ponds to rivers. Easily disturbed, it shows alarm by flicking its tail to display white outer feathers.

American Coot: white bill and small red forehead shield. **Ducks** have larger flattened bills.

Whitish bill and small red forehead shield.

Black head and neck. Dark gray elsewhere except for white on the outer undertail coverts. Has most improbable lobe-webbed feet.

More aquatic than the moorhen, coots favor wide stretches of open water in addition to marshes and ponds, including salt bays. Gregarious birds, they often flock in winter. Labored fliers, they skitter along water to get airborne.

Common Moorhen: white flank stripe, yellow-tipped red bill. **Ducks** have larger flattened bills.

Large black-and-white winged wading bird with bluish-gray legs.

Nondescript gray-brown above, paler below. Summer breeding plumage shows streaking. Bill is straight, fairly heavy and fairly long.

Rather local but numerous where it is found. Noisy and prominent, this species prefers marshes, shores and wet meadows. In the winter it is restricted to coastal regions.

Greater and **Lesser Yellowlegs**: dark-winged, yellow legs.

BLUE-WINGED TEAL

♀

♂

Pale blue on forewing, male with prominent white crescent on face.

Small. Green speculum behind blue forewing. The outer wing is gray-brown. The male has a gray head, and a white band before the black undertail coverts. The female is predominantly brown although belly is pale, unlike the male.

Favors marshes and ponds in summer. Winters in the south and South America. This species gathers and flies in flocks, rising straight from the water surface when disturbed.

Northern Shoveler: pale blue forewing, spatulate bill. **Green-winged Teal:** also has a green speculum but lacks blue forewing.

LAUGHING GULL
16½in RESIDENT/SUMMER V.

Adults have dark gray wings tipped with solid black.

The back is dark gray, the feet are black. In summer this species is black-headed with a red bill, otherwise white. In winter the head is a dirty white and the bill black. Immatures are varying browns with solid black-tipped wings.

The name is due to its harsh cry. A common coastal bird, predominantly of the east coast, it ventures inland infrequently.

Ring-billed Gull: paler gray back and wings, the latter black-tipped with white spots. **Bonaparte's Gull:** smaller. Pale gray back, red legs. **Western/Great Black-backed Gull:** much larger. **Terns:** slimmer build, cleft or forked tails.

LESSER SCAUP

INTERNAL MIGRANT **17in**

The trailing inner wing only shows a broad white band in flight. Peaked head.

When close it may be possible to note the male's glossy purple head. He also shows a pale gray back and paler side. The female is mainly brown except for a white face patch.

Common, seen on most water habitats, often in flocks.

Other **Ducks** lack the white inner wing band in flight. Female **Merganser:** markedly crested.

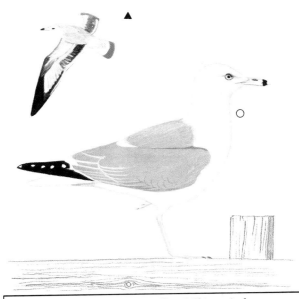

Adults have yellow legs. The yellow bill is entirely encircled by a black ring.

Gray back and wings, black-tipped with white spots. Head, tail, underparts are white, with the head brown-speckled in winter. Immatures show varying brown plumages for two years: dark bills. The light build identifies with practice.

An abundant species. Although common in coastal regions, it is also found inland around water, plowed fields and dumps.

(Adults) Other **Gulls** lack bill ring and yellow legs.
(Immatures) **Herring, Western** and **Gt. Black-backed Gulls:** larger and stockier. Other **Gulls:** smaller build, delicate bills.
Terns: slimmer build, cleft or forked tails.

WOOD DUCK

♂ ♀

Crested head and blue speculum.

Male: dark and iridescent above. Patterned green head, white collar, wine-red undertail coverts and breast, golden flanks, white belly. Female: teardrop-shaped eye patch. Otherwise dark brown, streaked below with a white belly.

A perching duck often seen doing just that quite high in trees where it nests. The trees need to be close to marshes, ponds or rivers. Call is a penetrating "hoo-eek."

Mallard: blue speculum edged with white on both sides. **Northern Shoveler:** green speculum and spatulate bill. **Red-breasted Merganser:** white speculum and crested head. **Green-winged Teal:** a small duck with a green speculum. Other female **Ducks** lack crest and white teardrop eye patch.

COMMON GOLDENEYE

Male: white face spot on green head. Female: dark brown triangular head, white neck, gray back.

Gray wings with square white patches very visible in flight. Male has an almost black back and tail with very white underparts. Female's tail is dark, paler underparts, a white belly and collar, and a dark brown head.

A sea duck, it summers on lakes, building its nest in nearby trees. Winter is spent either on the coast or large areas of inland water. Excellent divers: observers sometimes lose track of the bird as it travels great distances underwater.

Bufflehead: white face patch behind eye.

Long slender neck and gray bill; male with a long needle-tail, female shorter.

Brown-winged. Brown speculum, edged white. Male: chocolate brown head with a divider of white rising from breast. Gray-backed. Black undertail coverts. Female: predominantly brown, white belly.

Widespread on most areas of water, it is frequently seen in numbers in fields, grazing socially. A shy bird, it disturbs easily. Very rapid flight action.

Female **Ruddy Duck:** smaller, short-necked. Other female **Ducks:** lack slender neck and form.

Both sexes have twin-pronged crest and white speculum.

Male: glossy green head, white collar and streaked breast. Black above. Female: gray above with a rust-colored head. Both sexes have gray wings and tail with pale underwing and belly.

This species nests in wooded areas around northern lakes, but in winter migrates and may be seen on any body of water, fresh or salt, including sea coasts.

Wood Duck and **Mallard:** blue speculum. **Northern Shoveler:** green speculum and spatulate bill.

Very dark-bodied duck with a violet speculum.

Both sexes are virtually all brown. The head and neck are paler, and the female is consistently lighter than the male. The underwing is distinctively white in flight. Male has a yellow bill, female a green.

A wide habitat range from marshes and streams to lakes, rivers and estuaries. Interbreeding with the thriving mallard population is producing greater numbers of hybrids.

Mallard: blue speculum edged white on both sides.

Blue speculum edged white on both sides.

Male has yellow bill, glossy green head and neck. White collar and outer tail, chestnut breast, gray back and wings. Black curled tail feathers. Female has orange bill, whitish tail. Other plumage is a mixture of browns and buffs.

Both common and widespread, the mallard is likely to be found surface-feeding on any slow-moving freshwater body. Much domesticated, there are numerous varieties including the pure white.

Northern Shoveler: similar, but green speculum, spatulate bill. **American Black Duck:** violet speculum, edged white at rear only, if visible. **Wood Duck:** bluish speculum, crested head. **Red-breasted Merganser:** white speculum, crested head.

Adults have gray back, pink legs.

Adults: gray wings, white head, tail and underparts. A heavy yellow bill with red spot. In winter head, neck and breast become brown-speckled. Immatures show varying brown plumages and dark bills for three years. Very uniformly dark.

Although common in coastal regions, this abundant species is found inland as well. A raucous scavenger, frequently found at dumps.

(Adults) **Western/Great Black-backed Gull:** dark/black back and wings. Other **Gulls:** lack pink legs or are very much smaller. **Terns:** slimmer; cleft or forked tails.

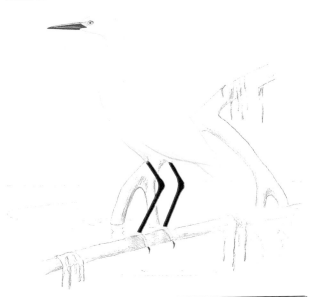

Black bill and legs, yellow feet.

Pure white. When breeding exhibits striking plumes from head, neck and back, the back plumes curling upwards. The feet become orange.

Plentiful in swamps, marshes and ponds shallow enough for it to wade. It disturbs its prey with its feet and then darts the dagger-shaped bill repeatedly into the water until the meal is secured.

Cattle Egret: legs pink, yellow or green. White form of **Great Blue Heron:** much larger; yellow legs. **Great Egret:** much larger; black feet.

Adults have black (very dark gray) backs. Pink legs.

Large gulls. Head, neck, underparts are white. Wing color same as back. Bills are yellow, red-spotted. Immatures have varying brown plumages and dark bills for three years.

Eastern and western coastal species respectively. True coastal species. Do not frequently wander inland.

Herring Gull (adult): pink legs, but back is pale gray. (Immatures): smaller, back and rump same color. Other **Gulls** are substantially smaller and have different colored legs. **Terns**: slimmer, cleft or forked tails.

Goose with white "chinstrap" and brown back.

Black head and neck. Brown wings and belly. Pale breast, white undertail coverts and upper tail. Black lower tail. Several subspecies with size decreasing northwards.

Our commonest goose. Widespread and often seen in flight in V-formation. Call is a noisy honking. Familiar on even quite small ponds, it settles on almost any body of water, and grazes on wetlands and fields in numbers.

Brant: white patch on neck, gray-brown back. **Snow Goose:** only similar in "blue phase" when whole head is white with gray-brown back.

Pied goose with "grinning" pink bill.

"White phase" is all white with just the primaries black. "Blue phase" has head and tail white, wing coverts blue-gray with the body and wings very dark. Immatures are brownish versions of each subspecies.

This species actually breeds on the Arctic tundra, but is widely seen on migration south. It winters on the Gulf coast in abundance, frequently with the two color phases together. Originally thought to be two separate species.

Domestic **Geese** are all white with orange bills.

112

Huge size and white head in adults. Immatures have white areas in inner underwing.

The adult is dark brown-backed with a very white tail and a heavy hooked yellow bill. Immatures are all dark, including the bill, for several years. The above-mentioned white areas are gradually replaced by the adult's dark plumage.

America's national bird, it is now regaining its numbers. Normally associated with rivers, lakes and coasts, it feeds mainly on fish.

Golden Eagle (adult): dark underwing, golden-brown head, (immatures): white underwing areas and primaries.
Vultures: small naked heads and shallow V-shaped flight attitude.

Black dagger-like bill, and glossy dark green head in summer.

Mostly pied plumage, a heavily checkered back, striped patch on neck, stripes into spots on flanks. White below, but other colors fade to gray in adults in winter and resemble immatures.

Loons have striking flight profiles, the neck and head being slung low. They are also noted for swimming low. Nest in wooded lakes giving remarkable yodeling call. Winter on the coasts.

Mergansers: smaller, slim hooked red bills. **Ducks:** smaller, flattened bills. **Cormorants:** hooked bills.

Large orange throat pouch.

Plumage is very dark green overall. The crests vary, being whitish in the west, dark in the east. Immature birds are brown above, paler below.

Widespread, often seen in numbers in flight with characteristic head up, bent-necked attitude. They swim low in the water and emerge to dry out with spread wings. Common coastally and inland around any major body of water.

Common Loon: black dagger-like bill, glossy dark green head without pouch.

Yellow dagger-like bill, long black legs and feet.

Pure white. When breeding, trails long straight plumes from back and neck.

Found in swamps, marshes, ponds and mud flats shallow enough for it to wade, it hunts its prey stealthily, leaning forward, quite unlike the smaller Snowy Egret.

Cattle Egret: legs and feet pink, yellow or green. **Snowy Egret:** black bill and yellow feet. White form of **Great Blue Heron:** yellow legs and feet; crested, larger.

Long black-streaked neck and black eye stripe to crest.

The white head, blue-gray back and wings (much darker trailing edge and primaries), yellow dagger bill and long legs make this a very distinctive species. The "Great White Heron" of Florida is an all-white subspecies.

Mainly solitary, it frequents most wet habitats, spearing fish from the shallows. In flight, slow wingbeats and neck tucked back make this an elegant bird.

None.

Black-chinned Hummingbird 3¾in

Blue-gray Gnatcatcher 4½in

Bushtit 4½in

Wilson's Warbler 4¾in

Black-throated Green Warbler 4¾in

White-eyed Vireo 5in

Chestnut-sided Warbler 5in

Black-and-white Warbler 5in

Warbling Vireo 5¼in

Bewick's Wren 5¼in

Bank Swallow   **5¼in**

Cliff Swallow   **5½in**

Field Sparrow   **5½in**

Purple Finch   **5¾in**

Least Sandpiper   **6in**

Ovenbird   **6in**

Semipalmated Sandpiper 6¼in

American Tree Sparrow 6¼in

White-throated Swift   **6½in**

White-throated Sparrow 6¾in

✏ Less Common Species

Hermit Thrush   **6¾in**

Lark Bunting   **7in**
♀ ♂

Semipalmated Plover   **7in**
♂

Orchard Oriole   **7in**
♀ ♂

Fox Sparrow   **7in**

Bobolink   **7in**
♂ ♀

Mountain Bluebird   **7¼in**
♂ ♀

American Dipper   **7½in**

Summer Tanager   **7½in**
♂ ♀

Western Kingbird   **8½in**

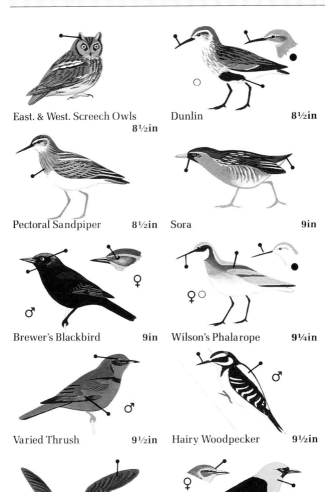

East. & West. Screech Owls

8½in

Dunlin 8½in

Pectoral Sandpiper 8½in

Sora 9in

Brewer's Blackbird 9in

Wilson's Phalarope 9¼in

Varied Thrush 9½in

Hairy Woodpecker 9½in

Whip-poor-will 9½in

Yellow-headed Blackbird 9½in

Less Common Species

Common Snipe   10½in

Lesser Yellowlegs   10½in

Black-bellied Plover   11in

American Woodcock   11in

Black-billed Cuckoo   11½in

Scrub Jay   11½in

Steller's Jay   11½in

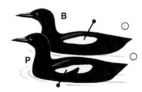

Black & Pigeon Guillemots   13 & 13½in

Greater Yellowlegs   14in

Bufflehead   14in

Less Common Species

Green-winged Teal   **14½in**

Ruddy Duck   **15in**

Short-eared Owl   **15in**

Prairie Falcon   **15-20in**

Common Barn Owl   **15½in**

Broad-winged Hawk   **16in**

Pileated Woodpecker   **17in**

Northern Harrier   **17-24in**

Sharp-tailed Grouse   **18in**

Black Skimmer   **18in**

American Wigeon **19in**

Green-backed Heron **19in**

Red-shouldered Hawk **20in**

Northern Shoveler **20in**

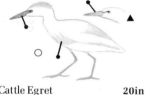

Cattle Egret **20in**

Barred Owl **20½in**

Caspian Tern **21in**

Canvasback **21in**

Osprey **21-25in**

Ring-necked Pheasant **21-35in**

Less Common Species

Greater Roadrunner   **22in**

Glossy & White Ibises **23 & 25in**

Brant   **24in**

Black-crowned Night-Heron
    25in

Glaucous-winged Gull   **26in**

Golden Eagle   **30-40in**

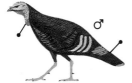

Wild Turkey   **36-46in**

Northern Gannet   **38in**

Brown Pelican   **48in**

Mute Swan   **60in**

Index and check-list

Keep a record of your sightings by checking the box.

☐ **Blackbird,** Brewer's 121
☐   Red-winged 37
☐   Yellow-headed 121
☐ Bluebird, Eastern 67
☐   Mountain 120
☐   Western 67
☐ Bobolink 120
☐ Bobwhite, Northern 42
☐ Brant 125
☐ Bufflehead 122
☐ Bunting, Indigo 60
☐   Lark 120
☐   Lazuli 60
☐   Snow 65
☐ Bushtit 118

☐ **Canvasback** 124
☐ Cardinal, Northern 35
☐ Catbird, Gray 36
☐ Chickadee, Black-capped 13
☐   Carolina 13
☐ Coot, American 96
☐ Cormorant, Double-crested 115
☐ Cowbird, Brown-headed 29
☐ Crane, Sandhill 87
☐ Creeper, Brown 56
☐ Crow, American 49
☐ Cuckoo, Black-billed 122
☐   Yellow-billed 80

☐ **Dipper,** American 120
☐ Dove, Mourning 45
☐   Rock 47
☐ Duck, American Black 106
☐   Ruddy 123
☐   Wood 102
☐ Dunlin 121

☐ **Eagle,** Bald 113
☐   Golden 125
☐ Egret, Cattle 124
☐   Great 116
☐   Snowy 109

☐ **Falcon,** Prairie 123
☐ Finch, House 21
☐   Purple 119

☐ Flicker, Northern 48
☐ Flycatcher, Acadian 59
☐   Alder 59
☐   Buff-breasted 59
☐   Dusky 59
☐   Empidonax 59
☐   Gray 59
☐   Hammond's 59
☐   Least 59
☐   Western 59
☐   Willow 59
☐   Yellow-bellied 59

☐ **Gannet,** Northern 125
☐ Gnatcatcher, Blue-gray 118
☐ Goatsucker, see Nighthawk 39
☐ Goldeneye, Common 103
☐ Goldfinch, American 15
☐ Goose, Canada 111
☐   Domestic 112
☐   Snow 112
☐ Grackle, Common 46
☐ Grebe, Pied-billed 93
☐ Grosbeak, Black-headed 72
☐   Evening 31
☐   Rose-breasted 72
☐ Grouse, Ruffed 81
☐   Sharp-tailed 123
☐ Guillemot, Black 122
☐   Pigeon 122
☐ Gull, Bonaparte's 92
☐   Glaucous-winged 125
☐   Great Black-backed 110
☐   Herring 108
☐   Laughing 99
☐   Ring-billed 101
☐   Western 110

☐ **Harrier,** Northern 123
☐ Hawk, Broad-winged 123
☐   Red-shouldered 124
☐   Red-tailed 83
☐   Sharp-shinned 76
☐ Heron, Black-capped Night- 125
☐   Great Blue 117
☐   Green-backed 124

☐ Hummingbird, Black-chinned		118
☐ Ruby-throated		10
☐ Rufous		52
☐ **Ibis**, Glossy		125
☐ White		125
☐ **Jay**, Blue		44
☐ Gray		79
☐ Scrub		122
☐ Steller's		122
☐ Junco, Dark-eyed		23
☐ **Kestrel**, American		77
☐ Killdeer		43
☐ Kingbird, Eastern		33
☐ Western		120
☐ Kingfisher, Belted		91
☐ Kinglet, Golden-crowned		51
☐ Ruby-crowned		53
☐ **Lark**, Horned		70
☐ Loon, Common		114
☐ **Magpie**, Black-billed		82
☐ Mallard		107
☐ Martin, Purple		30
☐ Meadowlark, Eastern		75
☐ Western		75
☐ Merganser, Red-breasted		105
☐ Mockingbird, Northern		40
☐ Moorhen, Common		95
☐ **Nighthawk**, Common		39
☐ Nightjars, see Nighthawk		39
☐ Nuthatch, Red-breasted		11
☐ White-breasted		20
☐ **Oriole**, Northern		32
☐ Orchard		120
☐ Osprey		124
☐ Ovenbird		119
☐ Owl, Barred		124
☐ Common Barn		123
☐ Eastern Screech		121
☐ Great Horned		50
☐ Short-eared		123
☐ Western Screech		121
☐ **Pelican**, Brown		125
☐ Pewee, Eastern Wood		64
☐ Western Wood		64
☐ Phalarope, Wilson's		121

☐ Pheasant, Ring-necked		124
☐ Phoebe, Eastern		27
☐ Pintail, Northern		104
☐ Plover, Black-bellied		122
☐ Semipalmated		120
☐ **Quail**, California		42
☐ **Raven**, Common		84
☐ Redstart, American		57
☐ Roadrunner, Greater		125
☐ Robin, American		41
☐ **Sanderling**		89
☐ Sandpiper, Least		119
☐ Pectoral		121
☐ Semipalmated		119
☐ Spotted		88
☐ Sapsucker, Yellow-bellied		73
☐ Scaup, Lesser		100
☐ Shoveler, Northern		124
☐ Shrike, Loggerhead		74
☐ Siskin, Pine		54
☐ Skimmer, Black		123
☐ Snipe, Common		122
☐ Sora		121
☐ Sparrow, American Tree		119
☐ Chipping		16
☐ Field		119.
☐ Fox		120
☐ House		22
☐ Savannah		58
☐ Song		24
☐ White-crowned		68
☐ White-throated		119
☐ Starling, European		34
☐ Swallow, Bank		119
☐ Barn		66
☐ Cliff		119
☐ Tree		18
☐ Violet-green		18
☐ Swan, Mute		125
☐ Swift, Chimney		17
☐ White-throated		119
☐ **Tanager**, Scarlet		69
☐ Summer		120
☐ Western		69
☐ Teal, Blue-winged		98
☐ Green-winged		123
☐ Tern, Black		90
☐ Caspian		124
☐ Common		94
☐ Thrasher, Brown		78

☐ Thrush, Hermit 120
☐   Varied 121
☐ Titmouse, Tufted 25
☐ Towhee, Rufous-sided 71
☐ Turkey, Wild 125

☐ **Vireo**, Red-eyed 63
☐   Solitary 62
☐   Warbling 118
☐   White-eyed 118
☐ Vulture, Black 85
☐   Turkey 86

☐ **Warbler**, Black-and-white 118
☐   Black-throated Green 118
☐   Chestnut-sided 118
☐   Wilson's 118
☐   Yellow 14

☐   Yellow-rumped 61
☐ Waxwing, Cedar 28
☐ Whip-poor-Will 121
☐ Wigeon, American 124
☐ Willet 97
☐ Woodcock, American 122
☐ Woodpecker, Downy 26
☐   Hairy 121
☐   Pileated 123
☐   Red-headed 38
☐ Wren, Bewick's 118
☐   Carolina 19
☐   House 12

☐ **Yellowlegs**, Greater 122
☐   Lesser 122
☐ Yellowthroat, Common 55